Visual ⊕ Explorers

Extreme Earth

BARRON'S

Photo credits:

Images © dreamstime.com: icebreaker © 1971yes; destroyed road © Arturoosorno; landslide on whidbey island © Crystalcraig; fox glacier © Ego04713; melting iceberg © Elenathewise; amazoon river © Jlvdream; shield volcano © Juliengrondin; hurricane sandy © Marcelahirkova; tornado intercept vehicle © Maxym022; avalanche © Mtrolle; exploding lava (front cover) © Nopow; angel falls © Nordicview; pyroclastic flow © OnAir2; trango towers © Poendl; khumbu © Prudek; floods in calcutta, india © Samrat35; caspian sea © Ustinenkoav; earthquake (back cover) © Yekaixp. Images © shutterstock.com: mudpot (p1) © Filip Fuxa; ko tapu island © Agnieszka Guzowska; landslide in india © AJP; cenote © Ales Liska; tsunami warning sign © Alistair Michael Thomas; atlantic puffin © Allan Wood Photography; mount erebus © AndreAnita; women carrying water © Arapov Sergey; haiti © arindambanerjee; iceberg, iguazu falls © axily; death valley © Bill Perry; cinder cone © Billy York; dust storm © cholder; icebergs in greenland © Chris Howey; volcanic eruption (front cover) © Dariush M; ice cave (front cover) © Dean Pennala; sand dunes (back cover) © Denis Burdin; white desert © Dmitry Saparov; research station © Dmytro Pylypenko; strato volcano © Edwin Verin; puerto princesa © Ekaterina Pokrovsky; sand dunes in sahara © Eniko Balogh; fumarole © Filip Fuxa; crashing waves of hurricane Ike © forestpath; monument valley, gobi desert © Galyna Andrushko; stalagmites and stalactites © George Allen Penton; mud pool © gkphoto.it; shilin stone forest © gringo54; mudslide in costa rica © hagit berkovich; niagara falls © Igor Sh; hailstones © Jack Dagley Photography; grand teton peaks © Jerry Sanchez; zambezi river © Jiri Haureljuk; eyjafjallajökull © Johann Helgason; perito moreno glacier © Joshua Raif; volcanic bomb © Karol Kozlowski; andes © kastianz; river colorado, dead sea © kavram; castle geyser © Kenneth Keifer; volcanic crater (front cover) © Khoroshunova Olga; mont fuji © koi88; the wave (p.2-3), japanese macaque © kojihirano; lightning © kornilov007; rila mountain lake © maggee; luon cave © marcokenya; tornado destruction © Martin Haas; aletsch © Martin Lehmann; cave salamander © Matt Jeppson; ice berg (p32) © meunierd; hubbard glacier © Michael Klenetsky; tornado on plains © Minerva Studio; leopard seal © Mogens Trolle; everest © my-summit; thermal pool © Nelson Sirlin; crack in bridge © NigelSpiers; crater lake © Norikazu; karakorum mountains (back cover) © Patrick Poendl; giant's causeway © Paul Krugman; Lake superior © pavels; satellite view of typhoon © photobank.kiev.ua; group of penguins © Photodynamic; lady knox geyser © Pichugin Dmitry; vatnajökull © Piotr Gatlik; nile river © Przemyslaw Skibinski; hurricane from space (back cover) © razlomov; strokkur geyser © Robert Hoetink; mount etna © RZ Design; ice cave © S.R.Lee Photo Traveller; polar bear © Sergey Uryadnikov; cactus island © shinnji; collapsed bridge, hurricane andrew © spirit of america; coyote buttes © Sumikophoto; hurricane katrina © Tad Denson; geysers in eduardo avaroa national reserve © Vladimir Melnik; stromboli © Vulkanette. Images © fotolia.com: lightning (front cover) © valdezrl. Images © www.flpa-images.co.uk: san andreas fault © Kevin Schafer/Minden Pictures/FLPA.

Introduction

From deep underground caves and lofty mountain ranges to strange desert rock formations and the icy wildernesses of the polar caps, the Earth is packed with jaw-dropping natural wonders. And when faced with its terrifying might—an erupting volcano, a twisting tornado, or a catastrophic flash flood—who can doubt our planet's extraordinary power? But even the parts of our world that we see every day, and which seem so ordinary, such as a sandy beach, have been slowly shaped over millions of years and are no less impressive.

Contents

Read on to find out more about extreme Earth...

Volcanoes

Volcanoes are **dramatic** proof of the great forces at work beneath the Earth's calm surface. A **volcano** is essentially a mountain with an **opening** through which lava, gas, and rock **fragments** escape. They tend to be located where pieces of the Earth's crust, called **tectonic** plates, come together or move apart. This movement builds up **magma** and gas. The resulting explosions can be incredibly violent and often **deadly**. A volcano's shape is determined by its **eruptions** as the material it spews out **hardens** and forms new rock.

Facts and figures

Tallest volcano
The Ojos del Salado volcano on the border of Chile and Argentina is the tallest volcano at 22,615 feet tall.

Loudest eruption
The eruptions of Mount Tambora in Indonesia, in 1815, could be heard for hundreds of miles.

Most volcanoes
Indonesia has the most volcanoes in the world with more than 13,000.

Annual eruptions
On average there are between 50 and 70 volcano eruptions each year.

Most active
Mount Stromboli in Italy has been erupting nearly continuously for over 2,000 years.

Highest density
The Kamchatka Peninsula in Russia contains about 160 volcanoes. 29 of these are active.

Mount Stromboli is one of three active volcanoes in Italy

Did you know?

Volcanic bombs are pieces of lava that are thrown from an erupting volcano. A bomb can be the size of a small car and will sometimes explode from gas pressure as it cools.

On other planets

The tallest volcano in the solar system isn't on Earth at all, but on Mars. Olympus Mons is a giant volcano that rises to an elevation of 14 miles and is 340 miles across!

Undersea volcano

Many volcanoes are found under the seabed. After several eruptions, they grow above the water's surface and form an island.

In **1815** over **71,000** people **died** when **Mount Tambora erupted**.

Ash plumes

In 2010 Mount Eyjafjallajökull in Iceland erupted. Clouds of smoke and volcanic ash rose half a mile in the sky. Tiny pieces of rock and glass contained in the clouds can damage planes if they suck it into their engines. Most airlines stopped flying for at least six days until the clouds had dispersed.

Ash plumes from Mount Eyjafjallajökull

Pyroclastic flow

Erupting volcanoes throw out clouds of rock fragments and hot gas at high speed. It crashes down the sides of a volcano like an avalanche, reaching speeds of over 400 miles per hour. Pyroclastic flows are so hot and deadly that anyone caught in one will be killed instantly.

Burning rivers

Lava flows are made up of searing molten rock that is released from an erupting volcano. Everything in the path of a lava flow will be knocked over, surrounded and buried by lava, or ignited by its hot temperature. Deaths caused by lava flows are uncommon as most move quite slowly.

A house hit by a pyroclastic flow

Rivers of lava flow from Mount Etna

Fact file

Common types of volcano

There are three types of volcanoes that have different shapes and types of eruptions: strato, shield, and cinder cones.

Strato volcano
These steep, symmetrical volcanoes are usually the most violent. They are created when tectonic plates push together.

Shield volcano
Eruptions of thin, runny lava form these volcanoes. They are low, with gently sloping sides. Eruptions can be frequent but gentle.

Cinder cones
These are the most common type of volcano. They may occur alone or, more often, on the sides of strato or shield volcanoes.

Hot springs

Hot springs are further evidence of the awesome **power** of our planet. They occur where hot water **rises** on a regular basis to the **Earth's** surface from deep underground. The water can be emitted as a jet of **boiling** hot water and steam (a geyser) or can bubble up into a thermal pool. People have used hot **springs** and thermal pools for bathing since **ancient** times. Geothermal energy is also used these days to **generate** electricity. Other thermal features are fumaroles, where the water comes to the **surface** as steam, and **mudpots**, where the water is mixed with mud or clay.

Facts and figures

Number of geysers
It is estimated that there are about 1,000 active geysers in the world.

Tallest geyser
Steamboat Geyser in Yellowstone National Park blows water 300 feet high.

Highest density
Yellowstone National Park has the world's highest density of geysers and hot springs.

Largest hot spring
At 660 feet in width, Frying Pan Lake in New Zealand is the world's largest hot spring.

Deepest hot spring
The Great Pagosa hot spring in Colorado has a depth of over 1,000 feet.

Highest hot spring
The Yangbajain hot springs in southwest China are 15,000 feet above sea level.

Old Faithful

Probably the most famous geyser in the world is found at Yellowstone National Park. Old Faithful erupts about every 50–100 minutes.

Mineral packed

The water in a hot spring is rich in mineral salts. They dissolve from the rocks the water has passed through on its way to the surface.

About half of the world's geysers are in Yellowstone National Park.

Did you know?

Japanese macaques that live in the high mountains have discovered a way to keep warm in the icy temperatures. They bathe in the hot water of the thermal spas!

Geysers eject a column of water and steam into the air

Thermal pool in
Yellowstone National Park

Amazing geysers of the world

The term "geyser" comes from an old Icelandic word meaning "to gush," but there are geysers all over the world.

Castle Geyser
Castle Geyser was given its name in 1870 as it looked like a medieval castle, but its shape has since changed.

Strokkur
This fountain geyser in Iceland erupts every 4 to 8 minutes with a jet of water that can reach hights of 50−65 feet.

Lady Knox geyser
A soaplike substance is dropped into this New Zealand geyser's vent every day to make it erupt for crowds of tourists.

Thermal pools

The water in thermal pools rapidly comes to the surface from heated rock beneath the ground. As the water passes over this rock it collects different minerals. Brilliant colors often appear around the hot spring as different types of algae, minerals, rocks, and bacteria form rims around the pools.

Fumaroles

These vents in the Earth's surface can emit steam. They are found on or near active volcanoes. They expel steam rather than water because they are heated to a high temperature by molten rock several miles underground. The water turns to vapor before it escapes.

Fumarole in
Hverir, Iceland

Boiling mud

Mudpots, also called mud pools, are areas of hot bubbling mud. Unlike geysers and hot springs, mudpots have almost no water; instead, they release gases. The hot gases cause mudpots to bubble and burst and to create a plopping sound. The gases also make an unpleasant smell like rotten eggs!

Mud pool in
Emilia, Italy

Earthquakes

Powerful **earthquakes** can be bad news for the people who live near them, especially in built-up areas like **cities**, where they can cause a huge amount of **devastation** to buildings and structures. An earthquake, sometimes called a **tremor**, is most often linked to the movement of a **fault**, which rapidly releases **energy** into the Earth's crust. What this means is that the ground shakes and shifts—often **violently**, depending on the magnitude of the **quake**. Though there are several million earthquakes a year, fewer than three will be higher than 9 on the **Richter** scale.

Facts and figures

Highest magnitude
The Temuco–Valdivia earthquake in Chile, May 1960, measured 9.5 on the Richter scale.

Annual earthquakes
On average there are about 3 million earthquakes in the world each year.

Deadliest earthquake
There were about 316,000 deaths caused by the Haiti earthquake in January 2010.

Longest duration
The Sumatran–Andaman earthquake in 2004 was the longest recorded earthquake at between 8 and 10 minutes.

Risky city
Kathmandu in Nepal is thought to be the city with the highest risk of earthquakes.

Worst damage
The 2011 Honshu earthquake caused 210 billion dollars' worth of damage in Japan.

Frantic animals

Scientists believe some animals behave strangely before an earthquake because they can sense the first tiny tremors.

Richter scale

Earthquakes are graded according to the energy released using the Richter scale. Quakes up to 3 are considered weak, but any above 7 can cause serious damage.

There are thousands of small earthquakes every day across the world.

An earthquake caused a huge crack in this bridge

Did you know?

Earthquakes can cause large amounts of water to shift, causing a tsunami. These fast-moving waves can be dozens of feet tall and create devastation when they reach land.

Destroyed city

In 2010 a devastating earthquake tore through Haiti in the Caribbean. Many buildings collapsed, hospitals were destroyed, as were countless homes. Over 316,000 people are known to have died. Experts believe that this was the worst earthquake in the region in more than 200 years.

Debris and rubble in Port-Au-Prince, Haiti

A collapsed bridge in California, USA

The San Andreas Fault

Broken bridges

A powerful earthquake can quickly destroy buildings and structures, such as bridges, shaking them to the ground. Engineers these days try to build earthquake-proof structures, with special features like shock absorbers, in areas prone to quakes.

Fault lines

A fault line is a mark on the surface of the Earth that traces a geological fault deep underground; up close it can resemble a crack in the ground or rock. The San Andreas Fault is a famous fault line that runs for more than 800 miles through California. This area of the United States is prone to earthquakes.

Fact file

How shock waves travel

The waves that are caused by earthquakes are called shock waves, and they can travel across the ground in four different ways.

direction of wave

Primary

Primary waves are the fastest waves. They travel at about 4 miles per second. They compress or stretch the rock in their path.

Secondary

Secondary waves shift the rock in their path up and down and side to side. They travel at about 2 miles per second.

Rayleigh

Rayleigh waves cause the ground surface in their path to ripple with little waves. They travel at about 2 miles per second.

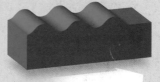

Love

Love waves are very destructive. They move in a zigzag motion along the ground at a speed of about 2 miles per second.

Deserts of the world

Though we tend to think of deserts as hot **sandy** places, these only account for about 20 percent of **Earth's** deserts. A desert is actually any very dry area of land that either doesn't get much **rain** or which loses more moisture through **evaporation** than it receives. Life is **tough** in a desert—because they are so arid, deserts can't support much **plant** life, and so animal and human life is limited too. Many desert animals are **nocturnal**, coming out at night when it is cooler. Deserts can be hot or cold, but even hot **deserts** with high daytime **temperatures** will be cold at night.

Facts and figures

Hottest desert
Parts of the Sahara Desert have reached temperatures as high as 134°F.

Largest hot desert
The Sahara is the largest hot desert in the world, occupying 5½ billion square miles.

Driest desert
The Atacama Desert in South America is so dry that some weather stations there have never recorded rain.

Coldest desert
Antarctica is the coldest desert on Earth. It is covered in ice and has reached temperatures of −128°F.

Most sand
Rub 'al Khali, at the center of the Arabian Desert, is the world's largest body of sand.

Densely populated
The Thar Desert in India is the most populated desert with around 83 people per sq km.

Did you know?

The Gobi Desert in China and Mongolia is expanding rapidly and grows by more than 1,500 square feet a year through the process known as desertification.

Sand dunes in the Sahara Desert, Morocco

Sahara Desert

The Sahara is the world's largest hot desert and one of the harshest environments on the planet. It covers most of North Africa and takes in 12 countries.

Giant dunes

The Sahara's sand dunes are 590 feet tall in places—that's higher than the London Eye!

A third of the Earth's surface is covered by deserts.

Cactus Island in Salar
de Uyuni, Bolivia

Salt desert

The Salar de Uyuni salt flats in Bolivia
in South America are the largest salt
flats on Earth. They were formed from
prehistoric lakes and are rich in salt and
other minerals. The salt crust is yards
thick in places and gives the landscape
an eerie flatness.

The White Desert

The enormous chalk formations in Farafra
in Egypt's White Desert give this place an
otherworldly look. They were formed when
the soft stone in a rocky plateau eroded,
leaving only the harder rock behind.
Scientists have discovered rock formations
very similar to these on other planets.

Fact file

Types of
sand dune

By using satellite and
aerial photography of
the world's deserts,
scientists have identified
five types of sand dune.

wind
direction

Barchan dune
These dunes are
crescent-shaped
individual sand mounds.

Parabolic dune
These dunes have crests
pointing upward and arms
that follow behind.

Star dune
These dunes have arms
radiating out from a central
pyramid-shaped mound.

Seif dune
These dunes have ridges
of blown sand that are
often several miles long.

The White Desert,
Farafra, Egypt

Death
Valley

America's Death Valley is
a below-sea-level hollow in
the Mojave Desert that is
surrounded by mountains.
It was named by prospectors
in the nineteenth century
who had to cross it to reach
the gold fields. It is well
named; a scorching 134°F
has been measured—the
world's highest recorded
temperature!

Death Valley National
Park, California

Transverse dune
These dunes form where
a lot of sand is blown by
wind in one direction.

The polar caps

The most **northerly** part of the world is the Arctic, a region covered in sea ice, glaciers, and frozen land. The most **southerly** region is **Antarctica**, an enormous ice-covered continent. The amount of ice in these areas varies according to the time of **year**, because in spring and summer some will **melt**. The only plants that are able to survive in the **polar caps** are small and tough, such as microscopic algae and lichen. Only **animals** that don't rely on plants for their food can **survive** in these barren areas, such as polar bears, **penguins**, and seals.

Facts and figures

Arctic temperature
The coldest recorded temperature in the Arctic has been measured at −90°F.

Antarctic temperature
The coldest recorded temperature in Antarctica has been measured at −128°F.

Arctic population
Approximately 4 million people live in the Arctic. Around half of this population live in Russia.

Antarctic population
The only people in this area are the researchers living at the scientific stations—less than 5,000 in total.

Arctic ice thickness
The average thickness of ice in the Arctic is 10 to 13 feet.

Antarctic ice thickness
The average thickness of ice in the Antarctic is 3 to 6 feet.

Continent of Antarctica

Antarctica is the fifth-largest continent in the world. 98 percent of its surface is covered in thick ice. The world's largest desert is located on Antarctica.

Arctic countries

The land in the Arctic region is divided among eight countries: Russia, United States, Canada, Greenland, Sweden, Norway, Finland, and Iceland.

Did you know?

If all the Antarctic ice melted, sea levels around the world would rise about 200 feet. Luckily the temperature in most parts of the Antarctic never gets above freezing.

A group of penguins gather on ice-covered rock in Antarctica

Polar bears and **penguins** never meet. Polar bears **live in the Arctic**, while penguins live in the **Antarctic.**

Mount Erebus on Antarctica

Frozen volcanoes

Antarctica is home to several volcanoes, most of them dormant. Only two of these volcanoes have peaks above the ice. The highest is called Mount Erebus and it stands almost 12,500 feet tall.

Greenland

Greenland is located between the Arctic and Atlantic Oceans. Over 80 percent of its land is covered in a thick ice sheet. The ice is believed to be an incredible 110,000 years old. Scientists have probed through the ice to a depth of 5,000 feet. By studying the DNA from the plants, trees, and insects they have found, they believe that there were once thick forests covering this icy land.

The ice shelf in northeast Greenland

A research station in Antarctica

Scientific research

There are currently over 40 scientific bases and 100 research stations on Antarctica. Scientists from all over the world come together to study the unusual icy landscape and the interesting wildlife. The hole in the ozone layer is another research focus for many of the scientists here.

13

Glaciers and icebergs

In very cold **environments**, nature makes great sheets of ice called **glaciers**. They are created when fallen snow does not melt. Over many years the layers of snow are **compressed** into large thickened ice **masses**. Glaciers flow like very slow-moving rivers. They advance down **mountain** valleys, across plains, or spread out to the sea. As a glacier **meets** the ocean, it forms a thick, **floating** platform called an ice shelf. As the ice is slowly pushed along the glacier, huge **chunks** will break free and float off into the ocean. These large pieces are called **icebergs**.

During the last ice age, glaciers covered a third of the Earth.

Glaciers worldwide

While most of the world's glacial ice is found in Antarctica and Greenland, glaciers are found in mountain ranges on every continent, even Africa!

Fox Glacier on the west coast of New Zealand

Water supply

Glacial ice is the largest store of freshwater on the planet, storing an estimated 75 percent of the world's supply.

Did you know?

Icebreakers are high-strength ships designed to break a passage through ice-covered waters. Icebreakers are used when a shipping route needs to be kept ice free.

The ice shelf of the Perito Moreno Glacier, Argentina

Amazing glaciers

Glaciers are among the most exciting features on Earth. These great rivers of ice sculpt mountains and carve out valleys.

Khumbu

With an elevation of 16,000 feet, Khumbu, in Nepal, is the world's highest glacier. It is also one of the most famous.

Aletsch

The Aletsch Glacier is the longest glacier in the Alps. Some of its ice is believed to have a thickness of over 3,000 feet.

Calving of the Hubbard Glacier, Canada

The ice shelf

Ice shelves are large permanent floating sheets of ice that are connected to land. They form wherever ice flows from land into cold ocean waters.

Calving

Ice calving is when ice breaks away from the edge of a glacier, and the chunks of ice that float away are called icebergs. These large pieces of ice detach from the glacier with a loud cracking sound. Some of the largest icebergs can measure up to 200 feet high and are several miles long. Ice calving often causes large, dangerous waves that have been known to flip boats over.

Floating ice

A huge iceberg in the Antarctic waters

An iceberg is a large piece of freshwater ice that has broken off a glacier or an ice shelf and which is floating freely in open water. Between 10,000 and 15,000 icebergs are calved each year. Some animals, such as polar bears, seals, and walruses, use icebergs as places to rest and hunt for food.

Vatnajökull

Vatnajökull is the biggest glacier in Iceland. This huge body of ice covers more than 8 percent of the country.

Mountains of the world

Mountains are magnificent **towers** of rock that dominate the land around them. They are formed by the **movement** of Earth's **tectonic** plates and rise when pieces of the crust come together, crashing or **folding** together, though volcanoes can also create them. Mountains are usually characterized by **steep**, sloping sides and sharp or slightly **rounded** ridges and peaks. The highest point of a mountain is its peak or summit. Mountains are **barren** places at these **chilly** peaks—with less oxygen and carbon dioxide up there, and little or no soil, there is **limited** plant and animal life.

Facts and figures

Highest peak
Mount Everest in the Himalayas has the highest peak at 29,035 feet tall.

From ocean floor
The highest mountain, from its ocean floor base, is Mauna Kea at 33,474 feet tall.

Longest system
The Andes mountain range stretches out for 4,350 miles, making it the world's longest mountain system.

Official smallest
Mount Wycheproof in Australia is the world's smallest registered mountain at just 485 feet tall.

Still growing
Mount Everest in the Himalayas is still growing at a rate of about 2.4 inches a year.

Mountain people
It is estimated that around 10 percent of the world's population live on mountains.

Did you know?

The Trango Towers are a group of mountains in Pakistan. The east face of the largest peak features the world's greatest near-vertical drop at over 20,000 feet!

Mount Everest is snow-covered all year long

The Himalayas mountain range was formed about 70 million years ago.

Danger mountain

Annapurna in Nepal is the most dangerous mountain to climb. It has been scaled by more than 130 people, but 53 have died trying.

Mount Chimborazo

The summit of Chimborazo, a volcanic mountain in Ecuador, is the furthest place on the surface of the Earth from its exact center, a distance of 3,967 miles!

The Andes

The Andes run along the western edge of South America. They are the oldest high mountain range in the world. They were formed just before the Jurassic period, around 199 million years ago!

Grand Teton

The highest peaks of the Teton Range, located in Wyoming reach a height of nearly 7,054 feet above the valley floor. These striking mountains were created around 13 million years ago when blocks of the Earth's crust began to shift. The area is now protected as an enormous national park so its great beauty can be enjoyed by many more generations.

An aerial view of the Andes

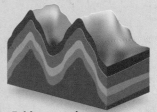

Fact file

How mountains are formed

Mountains can be formed by the slow movement of the Earth's tectonic plates, by erosion, or even by volcanic activity.

Fold mountain
When the Earth's plates collide, land between the plates is pushed up and the rocks fold, forming peaks.

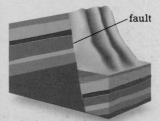

fault

Block mountain
Blocks of rock are sometimes pushed upward between faults to form a steep-sided peak.

magma

Dome mountain
When hot magma rises into the Earth's crust, it can push rock layers upward to form a dome mountain.

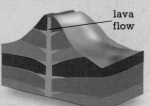

lava flow

Volcanic mountain
Repeated lava flow builds up around a vent in the Earth's crust to form a volcanic mountain.

Grand Teton National Park

Mount Fuji in Japan

Mount Fuji

Mount Fuji is the highest and the most famous mountain in Japan. Its peak stands 2.3 miles high and the mountain is a perfectly formed conical-shaped volcano. Mount Fuji last erupted on December 6, 1707, and it lasted till January 1, 1708. Mount Fuji is known as a symbol of Japan.

Weathering and erosion

Weathering and **erosion** work side by side to slowly shape the world's rock. Weathering is the constant process of **rock** being broken down and **sculpted** by wind and water, while erosion is the way in which the resulting **fragments** are taken away. These **natural** processes exploit the weaknesses within rock, because although most rock is hard it can be **shaped** over time. This is not quick; it can take **millions** of years. There are all sorts of **weirdly** shaped rock formations across the world—some of which are considered natural **wonders**.

Coyote Buttes is a sandstone rock formation located in the United States

Facts and figures

Giant's Causeway, Ireland
The 40,000 rock columns at the Giant's Causeway are believed to have been formed 60 million years ago.

Monument Valley
The tallest sandstone butte in this area is over 980 feet.

Coyote Buttes
1,000 dinosaur footprints have been found in this amazing sandstone landscape.

Wave Rock, Australia
This natural rock formation is shaped like a breaking ocean wave and is 328 feet long.

Uluru, Australia
At 1,148 feet high, this rock formation is one of the world's biggest.

Stone Forest, China
The beautiful stone formations, caves, and lakes of this park are believed to have been formed over the last 290 million years.

Rock lightning

The heat of lightning striking the sand on a beach can melt the sand to form a glassy rock called fulgurite.

Altering temperature

Frequent temperature changes can cause erosion. Rock expands when it is hot and shrinks when cold. Over time these changes can turn stones in the most arid desert into sand.

Did you know?

The 40,000 rock columns that form Ireland's Giant's Causeway are the result of an ancient volcanic eruption. It took millions of years of erosion for the columns to be revealed.

The Shilin Stone Forest in China

Acid rain

The Shilin Stone Forest, in China, contains some the world's most amazing rock formations. The stones are shaped like trees, mushrooms, towers, or pyramids. This landscape was formed by mildly acidic water washing through cracks in the rock until they became larger openings.

Flash floods

Monument Valley is a fascinating collection of rock formations. These strange formations began as sandy sediment in an ocean 270 million years ago. The relentless grinding of wind, rain, and floods wore away the layers of rock to leave the current shapes.

Monument Valley in the United States

Animal erosion

Animals can trample, crush, and plow rocks as they move around and burrow underground.

Plant power

Plant roots can break up stone by extending downward into rock cracks in search of water and nutrients.

Without weathering and erosion, the world wouldn't have any sandy beaches!

Breaking waves

Ko Tapu is a 65-foot-tall limestone rock, located off the shores of Khao Phing Kan on the west coast of Thailand. This peculiar-looking island was shaped by wind, waves, and water currents slowly eroding the rock. Ko Tapu is a part of Thailand's Ao Phang Nga National Park.

Ko Tapu island in Thailand

Flowing water

As well as being **necessary** for life, water is also a powerful force that **constantly** shapes the landscape. As rivers take fresh water across land to the sea, their water **erodes** the rock and soil of the **riverbed** and banks. When a river's flow is rough, usually because the riverbed slopes, which **creates** faster-moving water, the river may become a **rapid**. And when a river pours over a ledge of rock it becomes a **waterfall** or cascade. Such **spectacular** sights remind us that flowing water is packed with the energy **needed** to shape the world around us.

Facts and figures

Longest river
The river Nile is the world's longest river. It stretches for over 4,000 miles.

Most countries
The river Danube passes through 10 countries—more than any other.

Biggest river
South America's Amazon carries more water to the sea than any other river in the world.

Biggest waterfall
The world's biggest waterfall is Inga Falls in the Congo, where 84,540 cubic feet of water flow each second.

Tallest waterfall
The world's highest waterfall is Angel Falls in Venezuela, which is 3,212 feet high.

Widest waterfall
The Khone Falls in Laos is 6 miles wide, making it the widest waterfall on the planet.

Sacred river

The Ganges River flows through India and Bangladesh. It is sacred to people of the Hindu faith. Hindus bathe in its waters and worship the river as the goddess Ganga.

Several swimmers

There are over 3,000 species of fish living in the waters of the Amazon, making it the world's most bio-diverse river.

Did you know?

The Nile River was very important in the development of Ancient Egyptian society. Most of Ancient Egypt's historical sites are located along the banks of the Nile River.

A sharp bend in the Colorado River, Utah

The **energy** contained in **flowing water** can be **harnessed** to **create electricity.**

Running rapids

The Zambezi River is the fourth longest river in Africa. It stretches for around 1,550 miles. The river passes through flat sandy landscape and broad plains until it reaches the Ngonye Falls and rapids. This series of waterfalls and rocky terrain creates the most turbulent and fast-flowing part of the river.

A bridge over the Zambezi River

An aerial view of the Amazon River

The Amazon

The Amazon River runs through thick rain forest and out into the sea. It pushes over 24 million gallons of water out into the Atlantic Ocean every second.

Secret river

One of the most exciting and beautiful rivers in the world is located in the Puerto Princesa Subterranean River National Park in the Philippines. A huge cave contains a five-mile section of the Cabayugan River. This river runs through the mountains and out into the South China Sea. The dramatic caves are filled with countless enormous and beautiful rock formations as well as thousands of bats and birds.

Puerto Princesa Subterranean River

Fact file

Some amazing waterfalls

Waterfalls form in the upper section of a river. Flowing waters wear soft rock away, leaving a ledge for the water to run over.

Angel Falls
The tallest waterfall is Angel Falls in Venezuela. During dry months, most of the water evaporates before hitting the ground.

Niagara Falls
The Niagara Falls are made up of three waterfalls: the American Falls, the Bridal Veil Falls, and the Horseshoe Falls.

Iguazu Falls
These falls are located on the border of Brazil and Argentina. They are the result of an ancient volcanic eruption.

Lakes of the world

There are millions of **lakes** around the world of varying size and depth; the **largest** cover thousands of square miles. These **tranquil** expanses of freshwater are evidence of geological activity many thousands or **millions** of years ago. Lakes are always surrounded by **land** and are fed and drained by rivers or streams. They can also be supplied with water by **rain**, snow, **meltwater**, and water that seeps from the land. Lakes are mostly found in **mountainous** areas, where there has been glacial activity, but lakes can also be formed by **volcanoes**.

Facts and figures

Largest saltwater lake
The Caspian Sea in western Asia has a surface area of 230,000 square miles.

Largest freshwater lake
Lake Superior, between the U.S. and Canada, is the largest freshwater lake with a surface area of 51,000 square miles.

Deepest lake
With a depth of 5,370 feet, Lake Baikal in Russia is the world's deepest lake.

Longest lake
Lake Tanganyika in Africa is the longest lake in the world. It is approximately 410 miles long.

Highest lake
On the Argentina–Chile border, a volcanic crater lake stands 21,000 feet above sea level.

Most polluted
Due to nuclear waste storage, Lake Karachay in Russia has become the most polluted lake.

The Dead Sea is one of the world's biggest salt lakes

Salt lakes

A salt lake is a landlocked body of water with a high concentration of salts. When they have a higher salt level than seawater, they are called hypersaline lakes.

Lake Titicaca

There are 27 different rivers that feed Lake Titicaca. It holds more freshwater than any other lake in South America.

Did you know?

The Caspian Sea is classed as both a lake and a sea. It is huge and salty like a sea, but is an enclosed body of water like a lake. Even governments cannot decide which it is for certain!

Glacier lake, Rila, Bulgaria

Glacier lake

As ancient glaciers moved across the land they gouged large holes in loose soil or soft bedrock. But changes in the temperature on Earth meant that as these glaciers began to melt they filled the holes with water and turned them into lakes.

Crater lake

A crater lake is a lake that forms within a volcanic crater. If the lake covers an active volcanic vent, the water is often acidic and is saturated with gases and cloudy with a greenish color. Lakes that have formed in dormant or extinct volcanoes often have freshwater, which is exceptionally clear and clean.

A crater lake at Mount Zao in Japan

The **Dead Sea** in **Israel** is so **salty** that no **fish** are **able** to **live in it**.

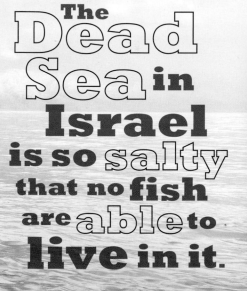

Lake Baikal

Lake Baikal in Russia is the oldest lake in the world. It was formed over 25 million years ago.

Lake Tahoe

Lake Tahoe contains over 32 trillion gallons of water. If it were ever drained, it would take over 700 years to refill naturally.

Lake Superior

The largest freshwater lake in the world is Lake Superior. The lake was formed over millions of years. Large areas of volcanic rock sank into the earth, creating a large basin. During the Ice Age this basin was filled with frozen water; then about 11,000 years ago the ice melted to form this lake.

The blue waters of Lake Superior

Caves

Deep, dark, and **underground** might sound spooky, but **caves** can be spectacular subterranean spaces! They are underground **chambers** that are formed by the natural processes of weathering and **erosion**, perhaps just by the constant **dripping** of water over many millions of years. Rainwater will seep into the small cracks in a body of **rock**, and its naturally occurring acid will slowly **dissolve** the rock, widening these cracks into **passages** and, finally, caves. Some caves contain **strange** rock formations or sparkling underground lakes.

The Luon Cave
(Tunnel Cave) on Bo Hon
island, Vietnam

Did you know?

The grotto salamander is a cave dweller. As adults they have pinky-white bodies with occasional orange spots. Their eyelids are fused shut, so they spend their adult life blind.

Animal species that live their life in caves are called troglobites.

Lava tubes

Unusual tube-shaped caves are formed by erupting volcanoes. The outer layer of a lava flow hardens to form a roof above the still-moving lava.

Mud caves

Mud caves were created by flowing silt from ancient lake beds, which has been eroded over time by wind and rain.

Cave sculptures

You will often see strange rock formations in caves. Stalactites hang down from the ceiling of caves, while stalagmites reach up from the ground. They are formed when water passes through the cave's cracks. Over many years the minerals in the water solidify to create these strange formations.

Cave with stalagmites and stalactites

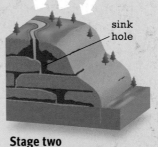

An ice cave at Fox Glacier, New Zealand

Glacier cave

Caves that are formed entirely from the ice of a glacier, though beautiful, are dangerous because of the shifting and melting ice. Such caves are formed by water running through or under the glacier.

Cave pools

Cenotes are freshwater sink holes that appear in caves in the Yucatán region of Mexico. They are formed when parts of the roof of a cavern collapses due to erosion. The water that collects in these amazing natural wonders is a crystal-clear turquoise color because it has been filtered through rock. There are believed to be about 6,000 cenotes in Mexico.

A Mexican cenote with clear blue water

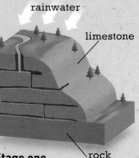
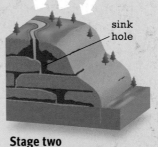
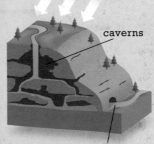

Shifting earth

A mass of snow, rock, or mud moving down a **mountain** or hillside can have a **devastating** effect on the surrrounding environment. Avalanches, rockfalls, and **landslides** often happen with little or no **warning**, and villages and towns can be buried. This **movement** of rock, snow, or soil can be the result of weather changes or the result of a more **dramatic** event, such as an **earthquake** or volcanic eruption. Sometimes human activity, such as mining, **deforestation**, and road **construction**, can also cause debris to fall.

Facts and figures

Mudslide
In February 2010, an enormous mudslide on the Portuguese island of Madeira took the lives of over 40 people and caused serious injury to 120 others.

Avalanche
In 1970, an earthquake in the Andes mountains set off a huge avalanche that destroyed the whole town of Yungay in Peru. It killed almost all of the town's 25,000 residents.

Landslide
In 1920, an earthquake triggered massive landslides at Kansu in China. Hundreds of small towns and tiny villages were destroyed and over 180,000 people were killed.

Rockfall
In 1960, at the Coalbrook mine in South Africa, a large rockfall caused 437 miners to be trapped underground. Most died of methane poisoning.

A bridge destroyed by a heavy landslide

Did you know?

When an avalanche happens, huge amounts of snow, ice, and rock fall down a mountain. A large avalanche can flatten villages and towns in a matter of minutes.

Snow speeding

The sliding snow and ice of a large avalanche can reach incredible speeds of up to 77 miles per hour.

Huge avalanche

In 1910 a huge blizzard struck the town of Wellington, WA. A thunderstorm unleashed an avalanche, sending a 10-foot wall of snow toward the town, killing 96 people.

Massive landslide on Whidbey Island

Shifting slopes

Landslides happen when rocks and sediment loosen and roll down a slope or cliff. Huge chunks of land can disappear in a matter of minutes. They can be caused by erosion from rain and wind, forest fires that burn the roots of plants, or earthquakes that shake the ground and break up earth and rock.

Falling rocks

Rockfalls happen when rocks break off from a cliff or slope and fall freely through the air. The stones may have been loosened by changing weather or by erosion over time. As the rocks reach the bottom they bounce and break, creating loose debris.

Landslides and rockfalls in India

Cutting down too many trees can loosen soil and lead to landslides.

Lethal lahars

The deadliest mudslides are called lahars. They are caused by volcanoes and can be very destructive.

Volcano danger

Volcanoes are prone to landslides, as they are made from layers of weak rock that tower above the surrounding landscape.

Mudslide

Heavy rainfall, melting snow, or floods may trigger the movement of soil and cause a mudslide. The mud separates from its base and will begin to move rapidly down a hill or slope. In extreme cases these rivers of mud will devastate whatever is in their way, and whole towns can be washed away and many people killed.

A severe mudslide in Costa Rica

Hurricanes and tornadoes

Hurricanes and tornadoes are **frightening** forces of nature, which may seem similar. Hurricanes, also called **cyclones** and typhoons, are **spirals** of thunderclouds that are fueled by the warm water in tropical seas. They gather in **ferocity** as they travel and can become enormous **storms** with violent wind, torrential rain, and lashing **waves**. Tornadoes, however, are thunderstorms that appear over land when warm and cold air **collide**. They form tall **columns** that stretch from the ground to a thundercloud. A tornado can cause terrible **damage** to anything in its path.

Facts and figures

Tornado outbreak
The biggest tornado outbreak occurred in April 1974 when 147 tornadoes touched down in the U.S. and Canada and claimed more than 300 lives.

Deadly tornado
In 1989, a 31-mile area of Bangladesh was savaged by a tornado. It has been estimated that over 1,300 people lost their lives and 12,000 others were seriously injured.

Mass destruction
In 1997, Hurricane Pauline wrecked buildings and made 300,000 people homeless along the Mexican coastline. Around 250–400 people lost their lives.

The Great Hurricane
In 1780, a hurricane devastated Puerto Rico, the Dominican Republic, the Lesser Antilles, and Bermuda. The death toll is estimated to be well over 22,000.

Did you know?

This Tornado Intercept Vehicle has been designed so filmmakers can shoot footage inside a tornado. The car features aluminium panels, stabilizing spikes, and a filming turret.

The spiralling clouds of a cyclone as seen from space

Hurricanes do not always reach land, but when they do they can be catastrophic.

Black tower

Most tornadoes start off as a white or grey cloud, but as they suck up more dirt and debris they often turn into black clouds.

Storm surge

A storm surge is often the most devastating part of a hurricane. It is created when a hurricane's wind spirals around to create a mound of water. If it hits the shore, it can cause terrible damage.

A tornado on the American plains

Tornado Alley

Most tornadoes in the United States are formed in an area nicknamed Tornado Alley. This area stretches through Texas, Oklahoma, Kansas, and Nebraska. The flat terrain, with warm humid air from the gulf of Mexico and cool dry air from Canada, creates perfect conditions for making tornadoes.

Killer twisters

Tornadoes are powerful forces that can cause the complete destruction of buildings and towns. Some of the most violent tornadoes have flattened homes, overturned cars, and ripped trees from the ground. People and animals are often killed by tornadoes.

Crashing waves

The combination of storm surge, fierce waves, and high winds can be deadly. Large waves have reached heights of over 23 feet and can span hundreds of miles. Hurricanes destroy buildings, cause beach erosion, and damage roads and bridges in coastal areas.

Tornado destruction in St. Louis, MO

Fact file

Devastating hurricanes

The violent winds, driving rain, and killer waves of hurricanes can cause severe damage to property and the loss of many lives.

Hurricane Katrina

In 2005, Hurricane Katrina killed over 1,800 people in the United States. The city of New Orleans was severely affected.

Hurricane Sandy

In 2012, the east coast of the United States was hit by Hurricane Sandy. The storm caused billions of dollars' worth of damage.

Hurricane Andrew

In 1992, this hurricane wreaked havoc across the Bahamas and the U.S. Winds reached speeds of over 174 miles per hour.

Hurricane Ike creating huge waves in 2011

Extreme weather

Unexpected hailstorms, **severe** flooding, and dangerous heat waves—**extreme** weather is simply weather that is different from the average pattern for that place or time of year. **Flash** flooding occurs when **low-lying** land is flooded rapidly. It can be caused by heavy rains or melting ice. **Global warming** is thought by many **scientists** to contribute to the growing frequency of this and other types of extreme weather, such as **forest** fires and dust storms, because the rise in the Earth's average **temperature** can increase the chance of such **devastating** events.

Facts and figures

Deadly drought
A Chinese drought in 1941 prevented crops from growing, and an estimated 3 million people died.

Flash flood
Over 1,200 people died in the flash floods that struck the southern Philippines in 2011.

Biggest blizzard
In 2008, a blizzard in Tibet dropped 6½ feet of snow, causing many buildings to collapse.

Dust storm
In 2009, an Australian dust storm measured 310 miles wide and 620 miles in length.

Fatal lightning
In 1971, 91 people died when lightning struck an airplane over the Amazon rain forest.

Forest fires
In 2008, a lightning strike started a forest fire that burned for 3 months in eastern North Carolina.

Did you know?

Hailstones are formed inside thunderclouds. They are mostly pea-sized, but can sometimes be the size of a golf ball! They can ruin crops, smash windows, and even kill.

Lightning strikes are giant sparks of electricity

Forest fire

When a heat wave or drought dries out the plants in an area, a fire can start and spread quickly. Forest fires can occur on every continent, with the exception of Antarctica.

Flash floods

Flash floods can be caused by thunderstorms that are concentrated on the same area or by heavy rain from tropical storms.

Rains cause floods in Calcutta, India

Severe flood

Most floods happen when excessive rain causes rivers to burst their banks, but they can also happen when high tides or gigantic waves sweep onto the shore. They can cause damage to property, pollute freshwater supplies, and spread disease.

Dust storm

Dust storms occur in dry areas where loose dirt can easily be picked up by strong winds. These winds swirl fine particles, such as silt, clay, dust, and other materials, to create a large, thick dust cloud. Poor visibility makes driving impossible. Dust storms may only last for a few minutes but often cause serious car crashes.

A huge dust cloud in Texas

Amazing lightning

Lightning is a buildup of an electrical charge. The strikes are just a few centimeters wide, but travel at 62,000 miles an hour!

Many storms

There are about 1,800 thunderstorms happening at any given time on Earth.

Each year about 24,000 people are killed by lightning.

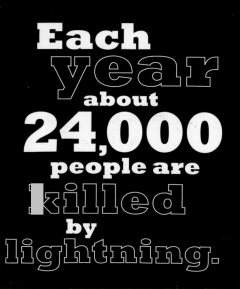

Women in Kenya carrying water

Major drought

A drought occurs when more water is used than is replenished by rain. The earth dries, water levels fall, and rain fails to come. A drought can cripple agriculture, greatly affecting communities who rely on farming, fishing, or herding. Droughts can lead to famines, war, and life-threatening diseases.

Glossary

Avalanche
A mass of snow, ice, or rocks that fall or slide down a mountainside.

Blizzard
A winter storm with strong winds and heavy snow.

Butte
A small, flat-topped hill in the desert.

Carbon dioxide
A colorless gas found in the atmosphere and absorbed by plants as they grow.

Crater
A hollow in the ground or in the top of a volcano.

Crust
The hard outer coating of the Earth that is made from rock.

Deforestation
The destruction of forests, for their timber or to clear land for farms.

Desert
A very dry place that has little rainfall.

Drought
A time of very dry weather when less rain than normal falls.

Earthquake
Sudden movements in the Earth's crust that cause the ground to shake violently.

Erosion
The wearing away of rocks by the weather.

Eruption
When a volcano explodes ash, gasses, and lava.

Evaporation
The process of a liquid becoming vaporized.

Fault
A crack in the Earth's crust formed by rocks shifting under the ground.

Flash flood
A sudden flood caused by a severe storm.

Freshwater
Water that does not taste salty. Rivers and many lakes contain freshwater.

Geothermal energy
Energy that comes from the heat in the interior of the earth.

Geyser
A hot underground spring that shoots out steam and boiling water.

Glacier
A huge mass of ice that slides slowly downhill.

Hurricane
A large spinning storm with very strong winds.

Iceberg
A massive floating body of ice broken away from a glacier.

Landslide
The movement of rock, earth, or debris down a sloped section of land.

Limestone
A sedimentary rock composed mainly of calcium carbonate.

Magma
Hot, molten rock underneath the Earth's crust.

Meltwater
Water released by the melting of snow or ice, including glacial ice, icebergs, and ice shelves.

Nocturnal
An animal that is active mainly at night and which sleeps during the day.

Richter scale
A system for measuring the intensity, or magnitude, of an earthquake.

Sand dune
A massive accumulation of sand, blown into a hill or ridgelike shape by the wind.

Stalactites
A spike made of stone which grows downward from the ceiling of a cave.

Stalagmites
A spike made of stone which grows upward from the floor of a cave.

Tectonic plates
The separate slabs of rock that form the earth's crust.

Tornado
A funnel of spinning air that forms beneath a thundercloud.

Tremor
A shaking or vibrating movement of the Earth.

Tsunami
A giant wave caused by an earthquake or volcano.

Weathering
The breaking up of rocks by wind, rain, or ice.

Index